Synthus Publishing

2013/14 Edition

Edexcel
AS Biology
Unit 2
Revision Workbook

revision academy

Samantha Richardson

revision academy

The Revision Academy

The company provides specialised revision that is specific to each exam within the following exam boards:
- AQA
- EDEXCEL
- OCR
- WJEC

We pride ourselves on attention to detail when it comes to revising and ensure that different learning styles are catered for.
The company currently delivers the following to help boost candidates grades:
- Workbooks specific to each individual exam
- One to one private tutoring sessions
- Intensive small group revision days specific to particular exams

For more information on these services visit our website at www.therevisionacademy.co.uk.

Samantha Richardson, a fully qualified Teacher, started the company in 2008. She has had many successes with her pupils since then and the company has grown steadily.
Samantha has a Masters degree from the University of Southampton and a Post Graduate Certificate of Education from the University of Cambridge. She has worked in both state and private schools and held the position of Head of Science before founding The Revision Academy.

Published by:
Synthus
29 Hickory Lane
Almondsbury
Bristol
BS32 4FR
UK   www.synthus.co.uk/publishing

This workbook has been written specifically to support students preparing for the Edexcel Specification AS Biology 6BIO2 examination. The content has been neither approved nor endorsed by Edexcel and remains the sole responsibility of the author.

revision
academy

About this book

The book contains many different revision techniques to help support you when preparing for the unit 2 exam.

The first section aims to check and test all of your basic knowledge of each topic. Here you should try to include all the key words and terms as they are vital to attaining full marks in exam questions.

The second section gives you space to keep all of your key notes on the most difficult topics of the module.

The third section highlights which subjects have been included in past papers so you may easily access questions on particular topics and give you a possible feel for what may come up in your exam.

The fourth section contains longer questions that require knowledge of several topics and how they are linked together.

The fifth section gives you examples of flow diagrams of all the key processes of the module.

The sixth section gives a list of the key concepts of the module that you can use to complete memory spider diagrams to check your current knowledge.

Finally the answers to all the basic questions and linked topic questions are included.

revision academy

Contents

revision academy

revision
academy

Basic Questions

This section contains questions on the basic knowledge you will need to know for each topic of the exam.

These questions are useful to answer a few times through your revision. We recommend you do them the first time using your text books and notes to help you and then answer them a second time using less help.

You can order additional copies of the questions by contacting us at info@therevisionacademy.co.uk.

Cell Ultrastructure

The Edexcel specification states the following learning outcomes for Cell Ultrastructure:

Candidates should be able to:

(1) **Distinguish** between eukaryotic and prokaryotic cells in terms of their structure and ultrastructure;

(2) **Describe** the ultrastructure of an animal (eukaryotic) cell (nucleus, nucleolus, ribosomes, rough and smooth endoplasmic reticulum, mitochondria, centrioles, lysosomes, and Golgi apparatus) and recognise these organelles from EM images.

(3) **Explain** the role of the rough endoplasmic reticulum (rER) and the Golgi apparatus in protein transport within cells and including its role in formation of extra cellular enzymes.

(4) **Describe** how the cells of multicellular organisms can be organised into tissues, tissues into organs and organs into systems.

revision academy

Cell Ultrastructure

1. What is **cell theory**?

....

....

....

2. How does an **electron microscope** work?

....

....

....

....

3. Describe the structure of a **transmission electron microscope**?

....

....

....

....

4. What is the difference between a **transmission electron microscope** and a **scanning electron microscope**?

....

....

....

....

5. What do the terms **resolution** and **magnification** mean?

....

....

....

revision academy

6. What are the basic differences between **eukaryotic** and **prokaryotic** cells?

....

....

....

....

7. What is **metabolism**?

....

....

8. What is a **cytosol**?

....

....

9. Describe the structure and function of the **nucleus**.

....

....

....

....

....

....

10. Describe the structure and function of **mitochondria**.

....

....

....

....

....

revision academy

11. Describe the structure and function of **endoplasmic reticulum**.

....

....

....

....

....

12. Describe the structure and function of **golgi apparatus**.

....

....

....

....

....

13. Describe the structure and function of **lysosomes**.

....

....

....

14. Describe the structure and function of **microtubules** and **centrioles**.

....

....

....

....

....

15. What are the key attributes of a **prokaryotic cell**?

....

....

....

The Edexcel specification states the following learning outcomes for Organisms from Cells:

Candidates should be able to:

(1) **Explain** the role of mitosis and the cell cycle for growth and asexual reproduction.

(2) **Describe** the stages of mitosis and how to prepare and stain a root tip squash in order to observe them practically.

revision academy

Organisms from Cells

1. What is the difference between a **unicellular** organism and a **multicellular** organism?

....

....

....

2. What is meant by the term **division of labour**?

....

....

3. How are **tissues** and **organs** different from one another?

....

....

4. What occurs during **interphase**?

....

....

....

....

5. What occurs during **prophase** of **mitosis**?

....

....

....

....

6. What occurs during **metaphase** of **mitosis**?

....

....

....

....

7. What occurs during **anaphase** of **mitosis**?

....

....

....

....

8. What occurs during **telophase** of mitosis?

....

....

....

....

9. What is **cytokinesis**?

....

....

....

10. How can the process of **cell division** be observed?

....

....

....

11. What is produced as a result of **mitosis**?

....

....

revision academy

12. Why are **daughter cells** identical?

....

....

13. When is **mitosis** used?

....

....

14. How is **DNA** arranged in the **nucleus**?

....

....

Reproduction in Organisms

The Edexcel specification states the following learning outcomes for Reproduction in Organisms:

Candidates should be able to:

(1) **Explain** the role of meiosis in the production of gametes and genetic variation through recombination of alleles and genes including independent assortment and crossing over (details of the stages of meiosis are not required).

(2) **Explain** how mammalian gametes are specialised for their functions.

(3) **Describe** the process of fertilisation in mammals and flowering plants (starting with the acrosome reaction in mammals and pollen tube growth in plants and ending with the fusion of the nuclei) and explain the importance of fertilisation in sexual reproduction.

revision
academy

Reproduction in Organisms

1. What is the difference between **asexual** and **sexual** reproduction?

....

....

....

2. What are the differences between **mitosis** and **meiosis**?

....

....

....

....

....

3. What aspects of **meiosis** give rise to **genetic variation**?

....

....

....

....

4. When do **mitosis** and **meiosis** occur?

....

....

....

revision academy

5. Describe the structure and function of a **sperm** cell.

....

....

....

....

....

6. Describe the structure and function of an **egg** cell.

....

....

....

....

....

7. Describe how **fertilisation** occurs in **mammals**.

....

....

....

....

....

8. What is **pollination**?

....

....

9. What is the difference between **self pollination** and **cross pollination**?

....

....

....

10. What are the names, structures and functions of the reproductive parts of a flowering plant?

....

....

....

....

....

....

....

11. How does **fertilisation** occur in flowering plants?

....

....

....

12. Why is **variation** important?

....

....

....

Embryo growth and development

The Edexcel specification states the following learning outcomes for Embryo growth and development:

Candidates should be able to:

(1) **Explain** what is meant by the terms stem cell, pluripotency and totipotency and discuss the way society uses scientific knowledge to make decisions about the use of stem cells in medical therapies (eg regulatory authorities relating to human embryo research, ability of stem cells to develop into specialised tissues, potential sources of stem cells, who could benefit from the therapies, procedures to obtain stem cells and their risks).

(2) **Describe** how totipotency can be demonstrated practically using plant tissue culture techniques.

(3) **Explain** how cells become specialised through differential gene expression, producing active mRNA leading to synthesis of proteins, which in turn control cell processes or determine cell structure in animals and plants (details of transcription factors are not required at AS).

(4) **Explain** how a phenotype is the result of an interaction between genotype and the environment (eg animal hair colour, human height, monoamine oxidase A (MAOA) and cancers), but the data on the relative contributions of genes and environment is often difficult to interpret.

(5) **Explain** how some phenotypes are affected by alleles at many loci (polygenic inheritance) as well as the environment (eg height) and how this can give rise to phenotypes that show continuous variation.

revision academy

Embryo growth and development

1. What is **growth**?

....

....

2. What is a **stem cell**?

....

....

3. What are the differences between **embryonic stem cells** and **adult stem cells**?

....

....

....

4. What is a **totipotent stem cell**?

....

....

5. What is a **blastocyst**?

....

....

6. What is **implantation**?

....

....

7. What is the role of the **umbilical cord**?

....

....

revision academy

8. What does the manipulation of **stem cells** give rise to?

....

9. Complete the table describing the diseases that **stem cell** treatment is used for.

Disease	Description
Type 1 Diabetes	
Spinal Cord Injuries	
Multiple Sclerosis	
Brain Damage	
Duchenne Muscular Dystrophy	
Cardiac Muscle Damage	
Burns	

revision
academy

10. Describe how **embryonic** cells are obtained from spare **embryos**?

....

....

....

....

....

....

....

11. Describe the other two sources of **embryonic stem cells**?

....

....

....

....

12. How can **adult stem cells** be obtained?

....

....

....

....

....

13. What does the **Warnock** report contain?

....

....

....

14. What are the arguments in favour of **IVF**?

....

....

....

....

15. What are the arguments against **IVF**?

....

....

....

....

16. What are the arguments in favour of the use of **stem cells**?

....

....

....

....

17. What are the arguments against the use of **stem cells**?

....

....

....

....

18. What is a **gene**?

....

....

19. What is **gene expression**?

....

....

revision
academy

20. What does the **lactose operon** do?

....

....

....

....

....

21. What occurs during the **lac operon**?

....

....

....

....

....

....

....

22. What is the role of **RNA polymerase**?

....

....

....

23. What is an **intron**?

....

....

24. What happens in the **nucleus** in the control of **gene expression**?

....

....

....

....

25. What happens in the **cytoplasm** in the control of **gene expression**?

....

....

....

....

26. What is **discontinuous variation**?

....

....

27. What is a **polygene**?

....

....

28. What is **polygenetic inheritance**?

....

....

....

29. How is height in humans controlled?

....

....

30. How is skin colour determined in humans?

....

....

....

....

revision academy

31. What else can influence human skin colour?

....

....

32. How does the **albino** form occur?

....

....

....

....

33. What affects animal fur colour?

....

....

....

....

34. What is a **tumour**?

....

....

....

35. How does a **cancer** arise?

....

....

....

....

36. How is the **cell cycle** regulated?

....

....

....

37. How can a **tumour** be initiated?

....

....

....

38. What is an **oncogene**?

....

....

39. What are **tumour suppressing genes**?

....

....

....

40. How are **viruses** and **cancers** linked?

....

....

....

....

41. What is **monoamine oxidase** and what is its significance?

....

....

....

....

The Edexcel specification states the following learning outcomes for Biodiversity-Plant Cells:

Candidates should be able to:

(1) <u>**Compare**</u> the ultrastructure of plant cells (cell wall, chloroplasts, amyloplasts, vacuole, tonoplast, plasmodesmata, pits and
middle lamella) with that of animal cells.

Biodiversity - Plant Cells

1. What is an **ultrastructure**?

....

....

2. What are the similarities do plant and animal cells have?

....

....

....

....

....

3. What are the differences between plant and animal cells?

....

....

....

....

4. What is the difference between a **chloroplast** and an **amyloplast**?

....

....

....

....

5. Describe the structure and function of a **chloroplast**.

....

....

....

....

6. Describe the structure and function of a **permanent vacuole**.

....
....
....
....
....

7. Describe the structure of the **cell wall**.

....
....
....
....
....

8. How is the **cell wall** formed?

....
....
....
....
....

9. What are the **middle lamella** and **lignin**?

....
....
....
....

10. What are **plasmodesmata**?

....

....

11. What is a **pit**?

....

....

revision academy

How the plant works

The Edexcel specification states the following learning outcomes for How the plant works:

Candidates should be able to:

(1) **Compare** the structure and function of the polysaccharides, starch and cellulose including the role of hydrogen bonds between alpha-glucose molecules in the formation of cellulose microfibrils.

(2) **Compare** the structures, position in the stem and function of sclerenchyma fibres (support) and xylem vessels (support and transport of water and mineral ions).

(3) **Identify** sclerenchyma fibres and xylem vessels as seen through a light microscope.

(4) **Describe** how to determine the tensile strength of plant fibres practically.

(5) **Explain** the importance of water and inorganic ions (nitrate, calcium ions and magnesium ions) to plants.

(6) **Describe** how to investigate plant mineral deficiencies practically. ;

revision academy

How the plant works

1. What is the role of the plant stem?

....

....

2. What are the roles of the plants leaves?

....

....

....

3. What are the roles of the plants roots?

....

....

4. What is a **tissue map**?

....

....

5. Describe the structure of the stem.

....

....

....

....

....

6. Describe the structure of the leaf.

....
....
....
....

7. What is **turgidity**?

....
....
....

8. What are **parenchyma**?

....
....
....
....

9. What is **collenchyma**?

....
....
....
....

10. Describe the structure of **xylem vessels**.

....
....
....
....

11. Describe the structure of **fibres**.

....

....

....

....

12. What is the difference between a **dicotyledonous** and a **monocotyledonous** plant?

....

....

....

....

13. Why is water so important in plants?

....

....

....

....

14. What is the role of the **cuticle**?

....

....

....

....

15. What is the role of **stomata**?

....

....

....

....

16. How is water taken up by plants?

....

....

....

....

....

....

....

....

17. What is **transpiration**?

....

....

....

18. What are **inorganic ions** used for in plants?

....

....

....

....

The Edexcel specification states the following learning outcomes for How plants are used:

Candidates should be able to:

(1) **Explain** how the arrangement of cellulose microfibrils in plant cell walls and secondary thickening contribute to the physical properties of plant fibres, which can be exploited by humans.

(2) **Describe** how the uses of plant fibres and starch may contribute to sustainability, eg plant-based products to replace oil-based plastics.

(3) **Describe** how to investigate the antimicrobial properties of plants.

(4) **Compare** historic drug testing with contemporary drug testing protocols, eg William Withering's digitalis soup; double blind trials; placebo; three-phased testing.

revision academy

How plants are used

1. How are plants linked with **fossil fuels**?

....

....

....

....

2. What are plants used for?

....

....

....

....

3. What are the different **plant fibres**?

....

....

....

....

4. What can the different **plant fibres** be used for?

....

....

....

....

5. How can **starch** be used?

....

....

....

....

6. What is significant about **bracken**?

....

....

....

....

7. What is **pyrethrum** and what is it used for?

....

....

....

....

8. What examples have been found in plants with **antimicrobial** properties?

....

....

....

....

9. How can plants be used in medicine?

....

....

....

....

revision
academy

10. Describe how drugs are tested before they are widely used.

....

....

....

....

....

....

....

11. Describe **William Withering's** work.

....

....

....

....

....

....

....

revision academy

The Environment and Biodiversity

The Edexcel specification states the following learning outcomes for The Environment and Biodiversity:

Candidates should be able to:

(1) **Explain** the terms biodiversity and endemism and describe how biodiversity can be measured within a habitat using species richness and within a species using genetic diversity, eg variety of alleles in a gene pool.

(2) **Describe** the concept of niche and discuss examples of adaptation of organisms to their environment (behavioural, physiological and anatomical).

(3) **Describe** how natural selection can lead to adaptation and evolution.

(4) **Discuss** the process and importance of critical evaluation of new data by the scientific community, which leads to new taxonomic groupings (ie three domains based on molecular phylogeny).

(5) **Discuss** and evaluate the methods used by zoos and seedbanks in the conservation of endangered species and their genetic diversity (eg scientific research, captive breeding programmes, reintroduction programmes and education).

The Environment and Biodiversity

1. What does **biodiversity** mean?

....

....

....

....

2. What is a **species**?

....

....

....

....

3. What is **taxonomy**?

....

....

....

....

4. What is the **binomial system** of classification?

....

....

....

....

5. How are organisms named?

....

....

....

....

6. What are the names of the **taxa** for classification?

....

....

....

....

7. What is a **biodiversity hot spot**?

....

....

....

....

8. What does **endemic** mean?

....

....

....

....

9. What causes **endemism**?

....

....

....

....

....

....

....

10. What is a **habitat**?

....

....

....

....

11. What is the difference between an **abiotic factor** and a **biotic factor**?

....

....

....

....

12. What is the **Simpson diversity index** and what is it used for?

....

....

....

....

13. What is a **gene pool**?

....

....

....

....

14. What is an **inbreeding group**?

....

....

....

....

15. What does the term **ecology** mean?

....

....

....

....

16. What is a **niche**?

....

....

....

....

17. How do organisms physiologically adapt to an environment?

....

....

....

....

revision academy

18. How do organism behaviourally adapt to an environment?

....

....

....

....

19. What is an **anatomical adaptation**?

....

....

....

....

20. What is **natural selection**?

....

....

....

....

21. What is the evidence for **natural selection**?

....

....

....

....

22. What are the five kingdoms?

....

....

....

....

revision academy

23. What is an **extremophile**?

....

....

....

....

24. What is a **domain**?

....

....

....

....

25. What are the characteristics of the different **domains**?

....

....

....

....

....

....

....

....

26. What is **extinction** and what may cause it?

....

....

....

....

27. How is **extinction** rate affected by human population growth?

....
....
....
....

28. What is **conservation**?

....
....
....

29. What issues have the rainforests seen?

....
....
....
....
....
....
....

30. What is the **red list**?

....
....
....
....

31. What is **practical conservation**?

....

....

....

....

32. What are **nature reserves** for?

....

....

....

33. What is **ex-situ conservation**?

....

....

....

....

34. What is **in-situ conservation**?

....

....

....

....

35. What are the advantages and disadvantages of **ex-situ conservation**?

....

....

....

....

....

....

36. What are the advantages and disadvantages of **in-situ conservation**?

....
....
....
....
....
....
....
....

37. What are the steps needed in creating a **seed bank**?

....
....
....
....
....
....

Smart Notes

In this section all of the most difficult parts of the exam are considered and space is made available for you to record the most important information.

This can be done in note form, bullet points or diagrams. It is a useful way of keeping all your notes in one place so you may refer back to them easily if you need to.

revision academy

....

....

....

....

....

....

....

....

Meiosis

Fertilisation

....
....
....
....
....
....
....
....

revision academy

Plant Fertilisation

....

....

....

....

....

....

....

....

Stem Cells

....
....
....
....
....
....
....
....

revision academy

Lac Operon

....

....

....

....

....

....

....

....

Cell Walls

....

....

....

....

....

....

....

....

....

....

....

....

....

....

....

....

SMART NOTES

Drug Testing

....

....

....

....

....

....

....

....

Adaptations

....

....

....

....

....

....

....

....

Past Paper Contents

In this section we have reviewed all the available past papers for this particular exam and highlighted the topic of each question within each paper.

This will help you to quickly identify the past paper you wish to use to test particular knowledge of a specific subject.

The past papers can be accessed from the Exam boards website. Alternatively you may register with us and download them from our website www.therevisionacademy.co.uk.

Past Paper Contents

Date	Question	Content
Jan 2009	1	Micrograph of tissue, golgi apparatus
	2	Plant and animal cells, eukaryotes, mitosis
	3	How Science Works (HSW) on seed growth, inorganic ions
	4	Stem cells, gene expression,
	5	Sperm cell, fertilization, HSW on pollen tubes
	6	Sustainability, xylem
	7	Adaptation
	8	Species, genetic diversity, zoos
June 2009	1	Mitochondria, Bacteria
	2	Organs & tissue, organelles
	3	Adaptation, egg cells, antimicrobials
	4	Meiosis, root tip squash
	5	Pollen tubes, water in plants
	6	HSW on height of plants
	7	Drug testing, carbohydrates, plants in industry
	8	Protein synthesis, stem cells
Jan 2010	1	Multiple Choice questions (MC) on cells, ER
	2	HSW on genotype / phenotype, testing
	3	Plant tissues, transpiration, gene expression, tissue culture
	4	Mitosis, calculation question
	5	Sperm & egg cells, fertilisation
	6	Diversity, seed banks, zoos
	7	HSW, calcium in shoots
	8	HSW, bacterial growth
June 2010	1	Polygenes
	2	Stem cells, embryo research
	3	MC classification, cell wall
	4	Mitochondria, calculation question
	5	Starch, HSW
	6	Biodiversity, HSW, adaptations, species diversity
	7	Plant reproduction, HSW, pollen tubes

revision academy

Date	Question	Content
Jan 2011	1	MC on organelles, stem cells
	2	Drug testing, HSW
	3	Genetic diversity, seed banks, calculation question
	4	Meiosis, sperm cells, HSW
	5	Organs & tissues, cellulose & starch, xylem
	6	Cell cycle, mitosis
	7	HSW on plant fibres
	8	Phenotype, HSW, lung cancer
June 2011	1	Biodiversity, species, conservation
	2	Cellulose, HSW
	3	HSW on nylon, prokaryotes
	4	Root tip squash, mitosis,
	5	Genetic diversity, adaptation
	6	Domains, golgi, apparatus
	7	Stem cells
	8	Antimicrobials, HSW
Jan 2012	1	MC on mitosis study, root tip squash
	2	Adaptation
	3	Species richness, asexual reproduction, HSW
	4	HSW on pollen tubes
	5	Domains
	6	Plants in industry chloroplasts, xylem
	7	Antimicrobials, HSW
	8	MC on HSW
June 2012	1	Organelles
	2	Cellulose
	3	HSW on plant fibres
	4	Meiosis & HSW, cell specialisation
	5	Haploid, HSW, protein synthesis
	6	MC on drug testing, HSW
	7	Plant tissues, MC, HSW
	8	HSW on seed banks

revision academy

Date	Question	Content
Jan 2013	1	Prokaryotes & eukaryotes, organelles
	2	Fertilisation, stem cells
	3	MC on cell structures, tissues, cellulose & xylem
	4	Species richness, genetic diversity, seed banks
	5	Antimicrobial properties, HSW on bacterial growth
	6	Plant minerals investigation plan, HSW
	7	Adaptions, endemic, genetic variation
	8	Cell cycle, HSW, cell specialisation

Linked Topic Questions

Increasingly we have seen exam papers include questions that require knowledge across all topics within the unit and also from previous units.

Therefore we have come up with questions that link topics together and require real in-depth knowledge of the subject content.

These questions will really test your knowledge and your ability to apply it together with other concepts.

Remember to think outside the box, these are not just questions on one particular topic!

1. How does the structure of a **plant cell** relate to the structure of a plant as a whole?

....

....

....

....

....

....

....

....

....

....

....

....

....

....

....

....

....

....

....

....

2. How does **meiosis** help to maintain **biodiversity**?

....

....

....

....

....

....

....

....

....

....

....

....

....

....

....

....

....

....

....

....

....

....

....

LINKED
TOPIC Q'S

revision academy

3. How can **biodiversity** be increased?

4. Why are plants so important?

....

....

....

....

....

....

....

....

....

....

....

....

....

....

....

....

....

....

....

....

....

....

LINKED TOPIC Q'S

revision academy

5. Can **cell specialization** be used in medicine?

....

....

....

....

....

....

....

....

....

....

....

....

....

....

....

....

....

....

....

....

....

....

....

....

This section contains flow diagrams of the major processes within the exam.

These can be used to test your knowledge by covering up the flow diagram and trying to remember each step.

In addition, writing the flow diagram out as a paragraph, as you would in an exam question, can be a really useful revision technique.

This is a useful tool to cement your knowledge on some tricky processes.

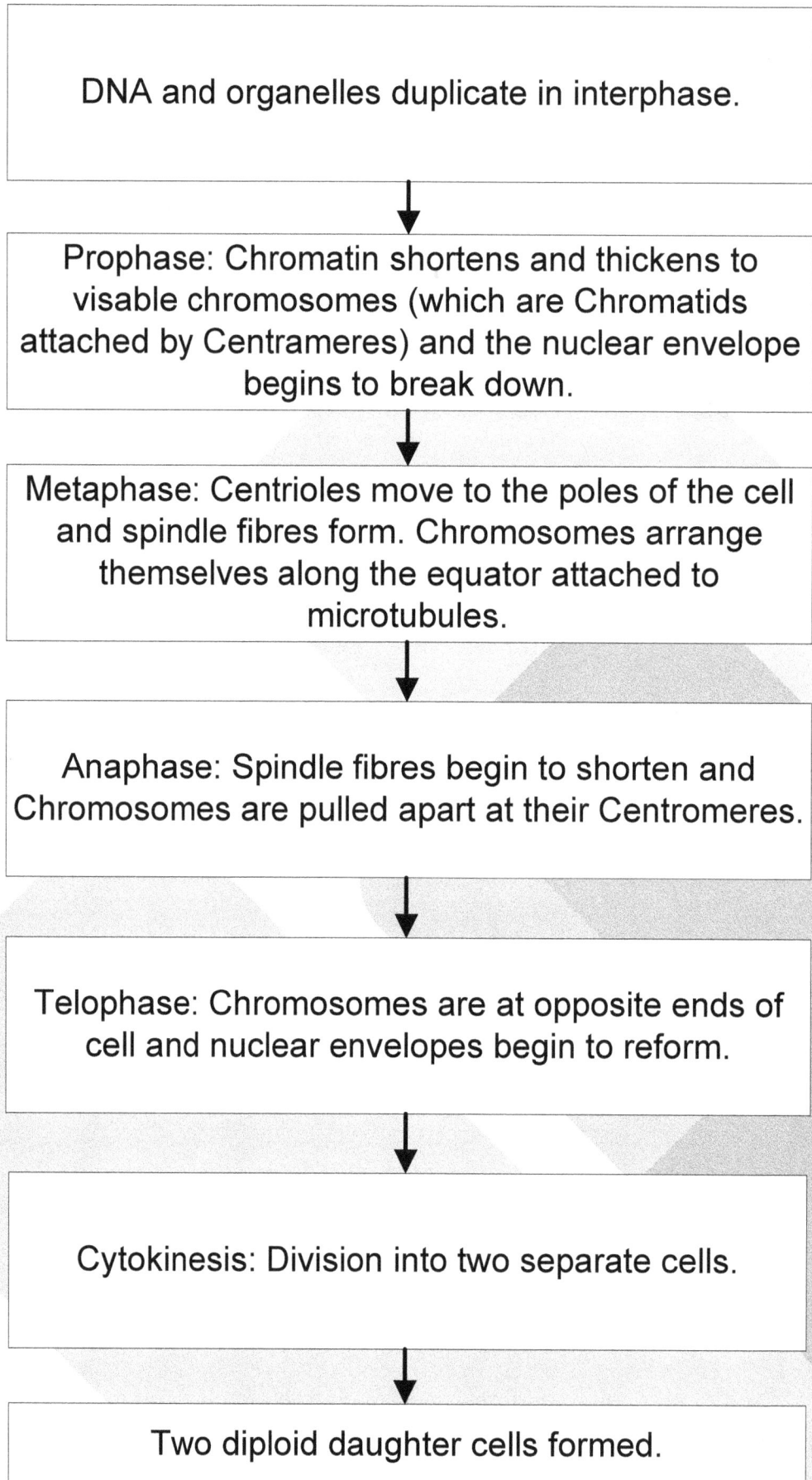

Mitosis

DNA and organelles duplicate in interphase.

↓

Prophase: Chromatin shortens and thickens to visable chromosomes (which are Chromatids attached by Centrameres) and the nuclear envelope begins to break down.

↓

Metaphase: Centrioles move to the poles of the cell and spindle fibres form. Chromosomes arrange themselves along the equator attached to microtubules.

↓

Anaphase: Spindle fibres begin to shorten and Chromosomes are pulled apart at their Centromeres.

↓

Telophase: Chromosomes are at opposite ends of cell and nuclear envelopes begin to reform.

↓

Cytokinesis: Division into two separate cells.

↓

Two diploid daughter cells formed.

revision academy

DNA and organelles are duplicated during interphase.

Prophase I: Chromatin shortens and thickens to visible chromosomes and the nuclear envelope breaks down. Homologous chromosomes pair up to form a bivalent.

Bivalent cross each other, where they cross is known as Chiasma. This is called CROSSING OVER.

Metaphase I: Spindle fibres form and bivalents line up at random on the equator. This is known as RANDOM ASSORTMENT.

Anaphase I: Spindle fibres shorten and bivalents are pulled apart breaking off at the Chriasmata.

Telephase I: Chromosomes are at the opposite ends of the cell and nuclear envelopes begin to reform.

Prophase II to Cytokinesis is the same process without crossing over occuring

Four haploid daughter cells are formed.

Meiosis

revision academy

Root Tip Squash

5mm of the tip of root cut off and kept.

↓

Tip is transferred to a watch glass with 30 drops of aceto-orcein and 3 drops of concentrated hydrochloric acid.

↓

Mixture is heated for 3 – 5 minutes.

↓

Tissues are placed on a microscope slide and mounted needles tease apart a root tip.

↓

More stain is added and a cover slip applied.

↓

The cover slip is squashed firmly but carefully and examined by light microscope.

revision academy

Sperm Cells formed in Testes in seminiferous tubules.	Egg Cells exist in the Ovaries as primary Oocytes from birth.

↓ ↓

Sperm Cells are immobile until activated during ejaculation.	From puberty secondary Oocytes begin to form.

↓ ↓

Sperms are introduced into the Vagina during sexual intercourse.

↓

Semen is ejaculated close to the cervix.

↓

The Vagina is quite acidic, but Semen is alkaline and neutralises acidity.

↓

The walls of the Uterus contract and this draws the Semen up through the Cervix.

↓

Sperm can swim into Oviducts

↓

Some Sperm reach a secondary Oocyte.

↓

Sperm pass between the Follicle cells surrounding the Oocyte and the Zona Pellucida (with the use of enzymes).

↓

When the enzymes have digested this it is called capacitation, this prepares the Sperm for fertilisation.

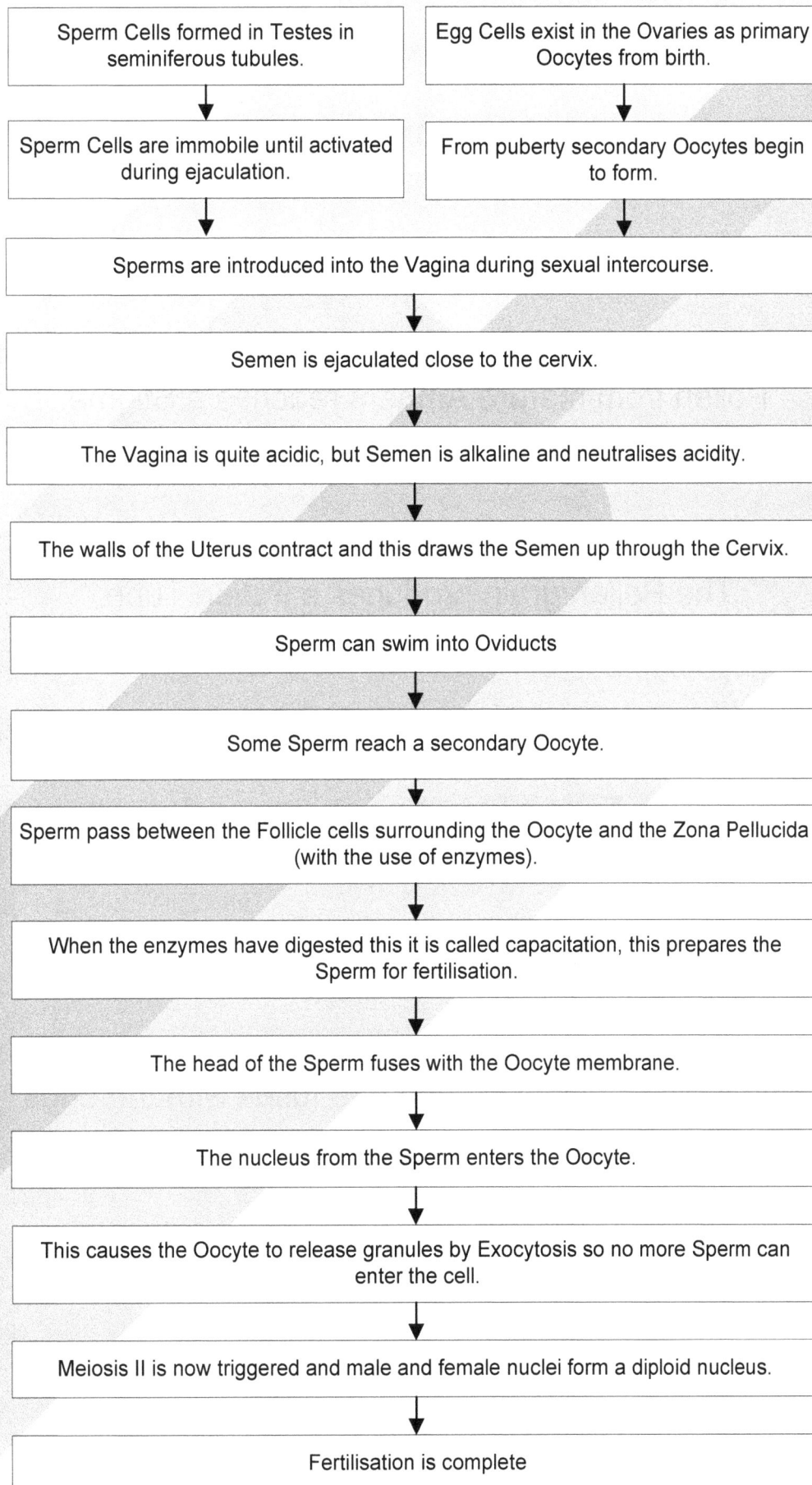

↓

The head of the Sperm fuses with the Oocyte membrane.

↓

The nucleus from the Sperm enters the Oocyte.

↓

This causes the Oocyte to release granules by Exocytosis so no more Sperm can enter the cell.

↓

Meiosis II is now triggered and male and female nuclei form a diploid nucleus.

↓

Fertilisation is complete

revision
academy

Fertilisation in Flowering Plants

Pollination occurs via Self-Pollination or Cross-Pollination.

↓

Pollen from mature Anthers reaches a Stigma.

↓

The Pollen grain produces a Pollen Tube.

↓

The Pollen Tube grows down between the cells of the Style and into the Ovule through the Micropyle.

↓

Two male Nuclei enter and one fuses with the eggs Nucleus and a Diploid Zygote forms.

↓

The other Nuclei fuses with another Nucleus and a food store begins to develop.

A follicle develops and Ovulation occurs.

↓

The cell is surrounded by Follicle cells

↓

The egg cell then gets fertilised by a Sperm and becomes a Zygote.

↓

The Zygote then moves down the Oviduct.

↓

The Zygote begins to divide in a process known as Cleavage. This is a 2 cell stage to a solid ball of cells.

↓

The cells then begin to organise and the Zygote becomes a Blastocyst.

↓

The Blastocyst embeds itself in the Uterine Wall in a process called IMPLANTATION.

↓

After seven weeks the implanted Blastocyst becomes a Foetus.

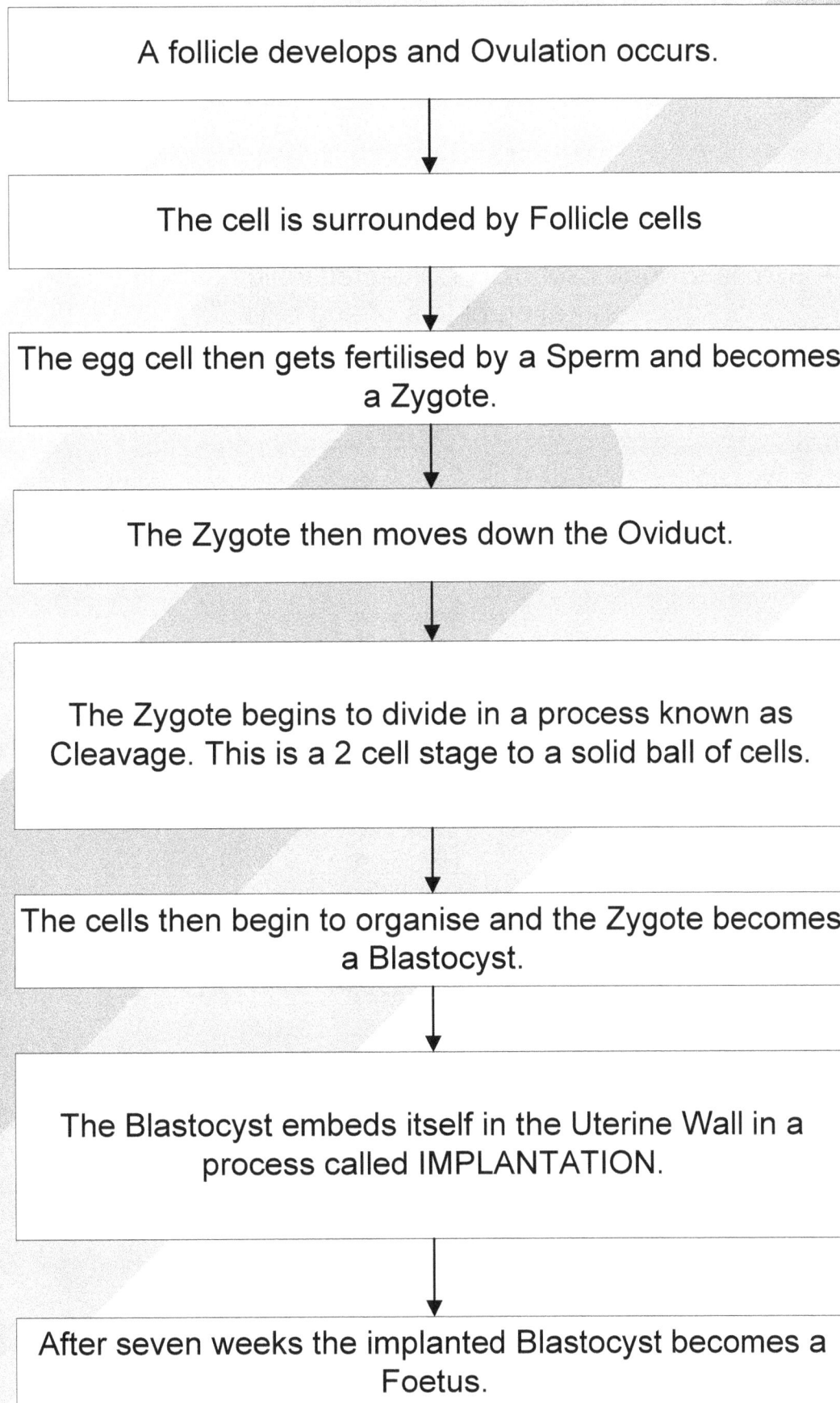

FLOW
DIAGRAMS

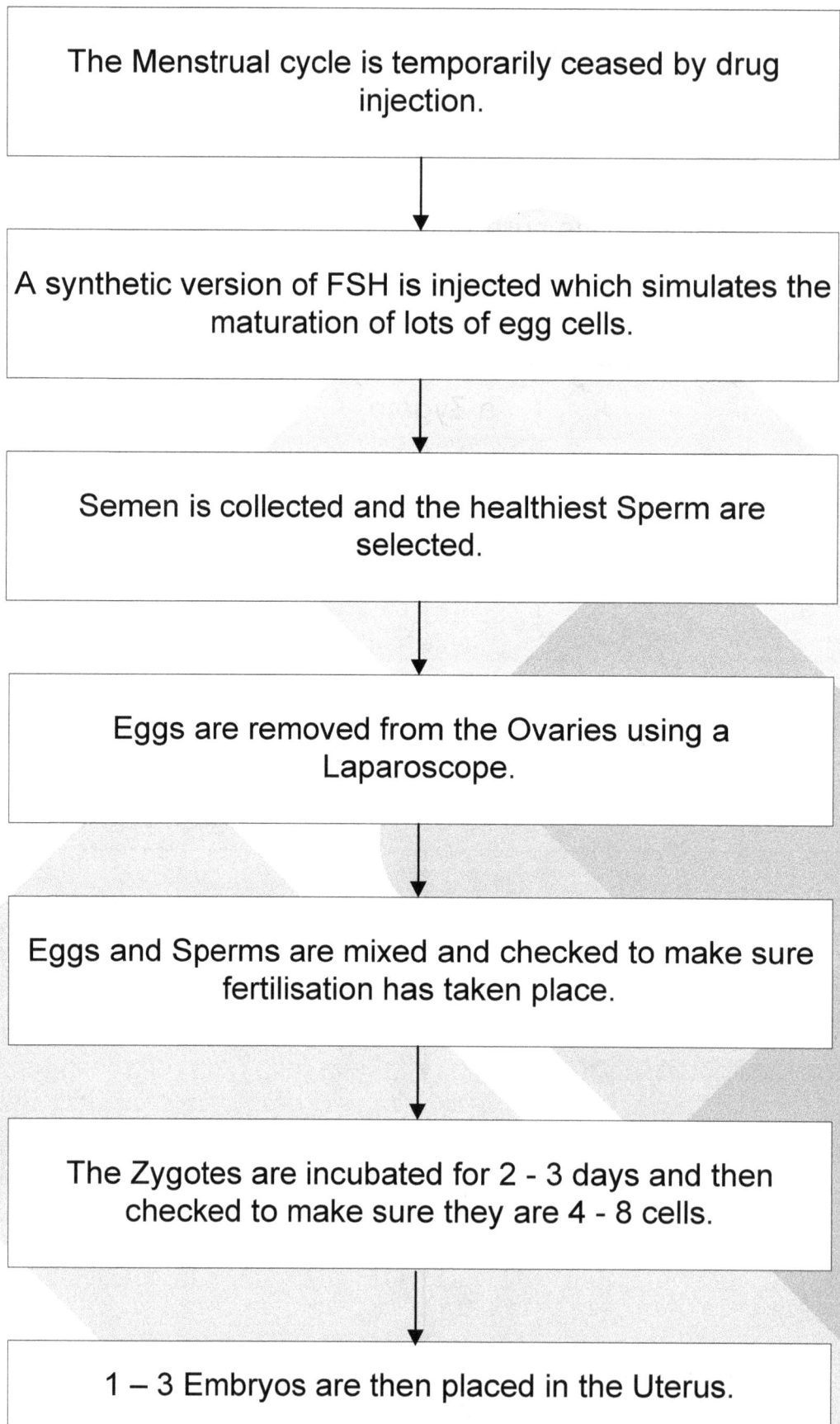

IVF

The Menstrual cycle is temporarily ceased by drug injection.

↓

A synthetic version of FSH is injected which simulates the maturation of lots of egg cells.

↓

Semen is collected and the healthiest Sperm are selected.

↓

Eggs are removed from the Ovaries using a Laparoscope.

↓

Eggs and Sperms are mixed and checked to make sure fertilisation has taken place.

↓

The Zygotes are incubated for 2 - 3 days and then checked to make sure they are 4 - 8 cells.

↓

1 – 3 Embryos are then placed in the Uterus.

revision
academy

Embryo from IVF.

↓

One cell is removed from the Embryo.

↓

The Embryo is the implanted in the Uterus.

↓

The single cell that was removed undergoes Mitosis.

↓

One daughter cell is grown in a culture for ES cells.

↓

The other cell is used for pre-implantation genetic diagnosis.

Obtaining Embryo Stem Cells

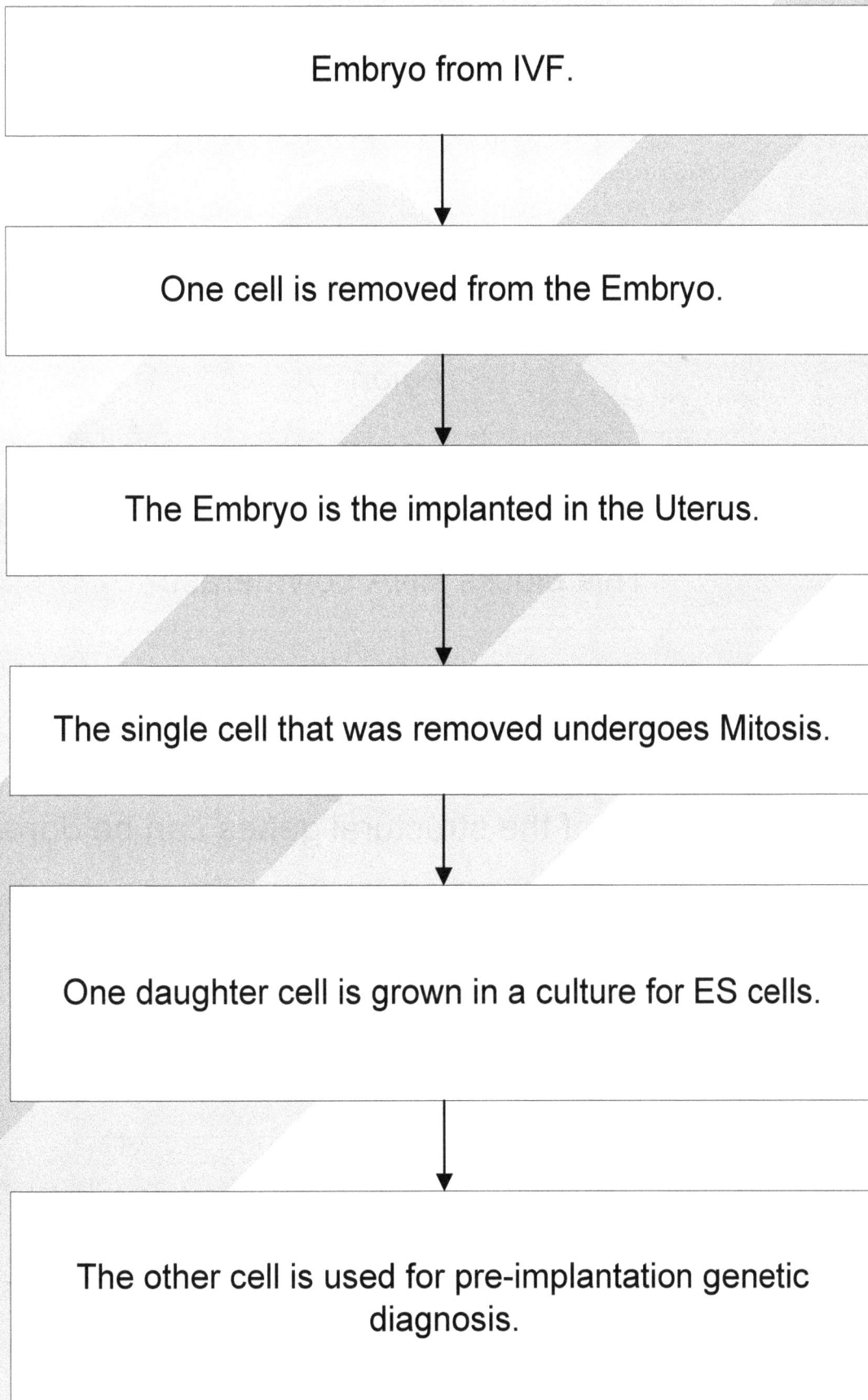

The Lac operon: Lactose Absent

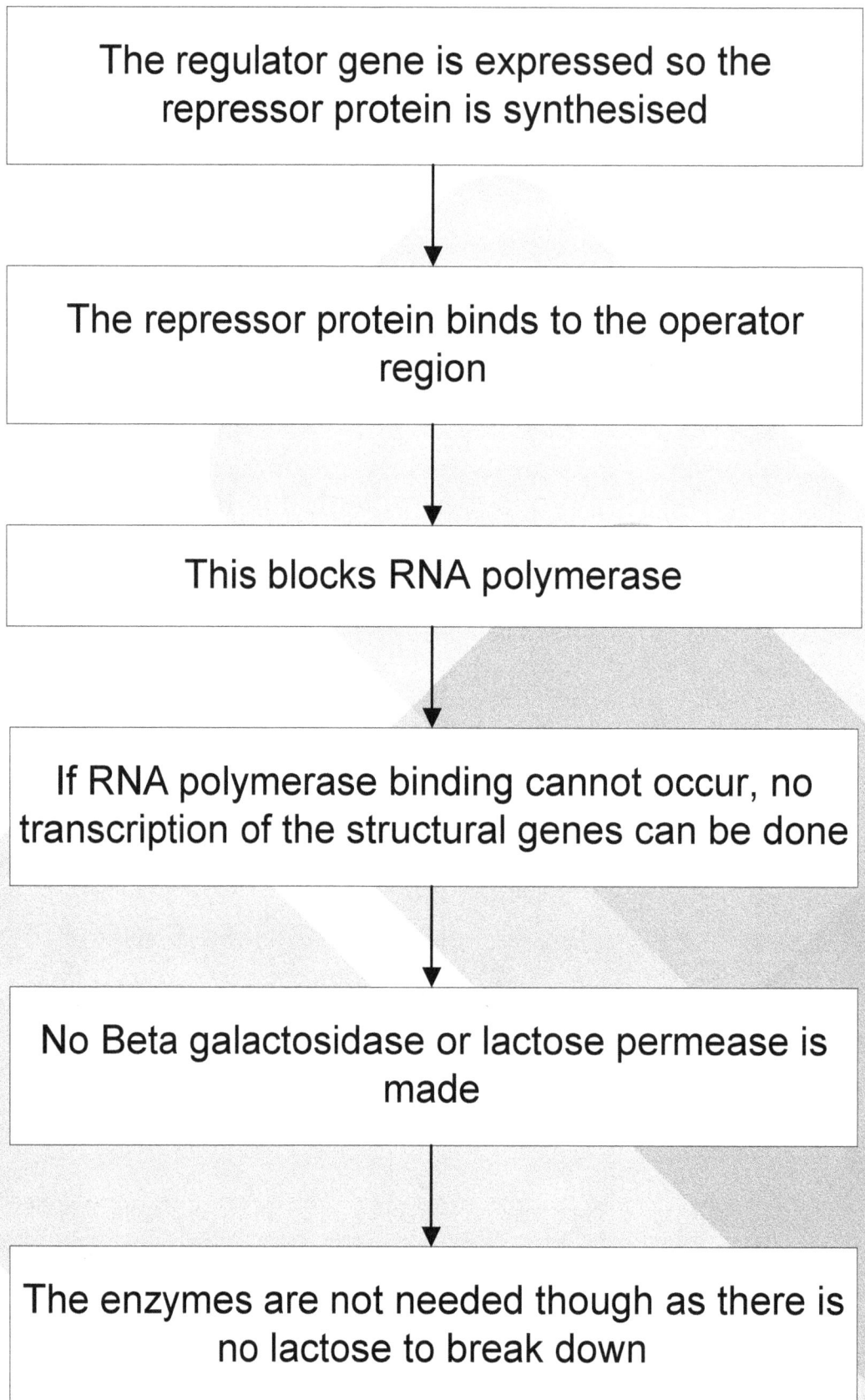

The regulator gene is expressed so the repressor protein is synthesised

↓

The repressor protein binds to the operator region

↓

This blocks RNA polymerase

↓

If RNA polymerase binding cannot occur, no transcription of the structural genes can be done

↓

No Beta galactosidase or lactose permease is made

↓

The enzymes are not needed though as there is no lactose to break down

revision academy

The regulator gene is expressed so the repressor protein is synthesised

↓

Any lactose present will bind to the repressor protein

↓

This changes the shape of the repressor protein

↓

The repressor protein cannot bind to the operator region

↓

The promoter and operator regions are now unblocked

↓

RNA polymerase can synthesise Beta galactosidase and lactose permease

↓

These enzymes are now available to break lactose into glucose and galactose for respiration

The Lac Operon: Lactose Present

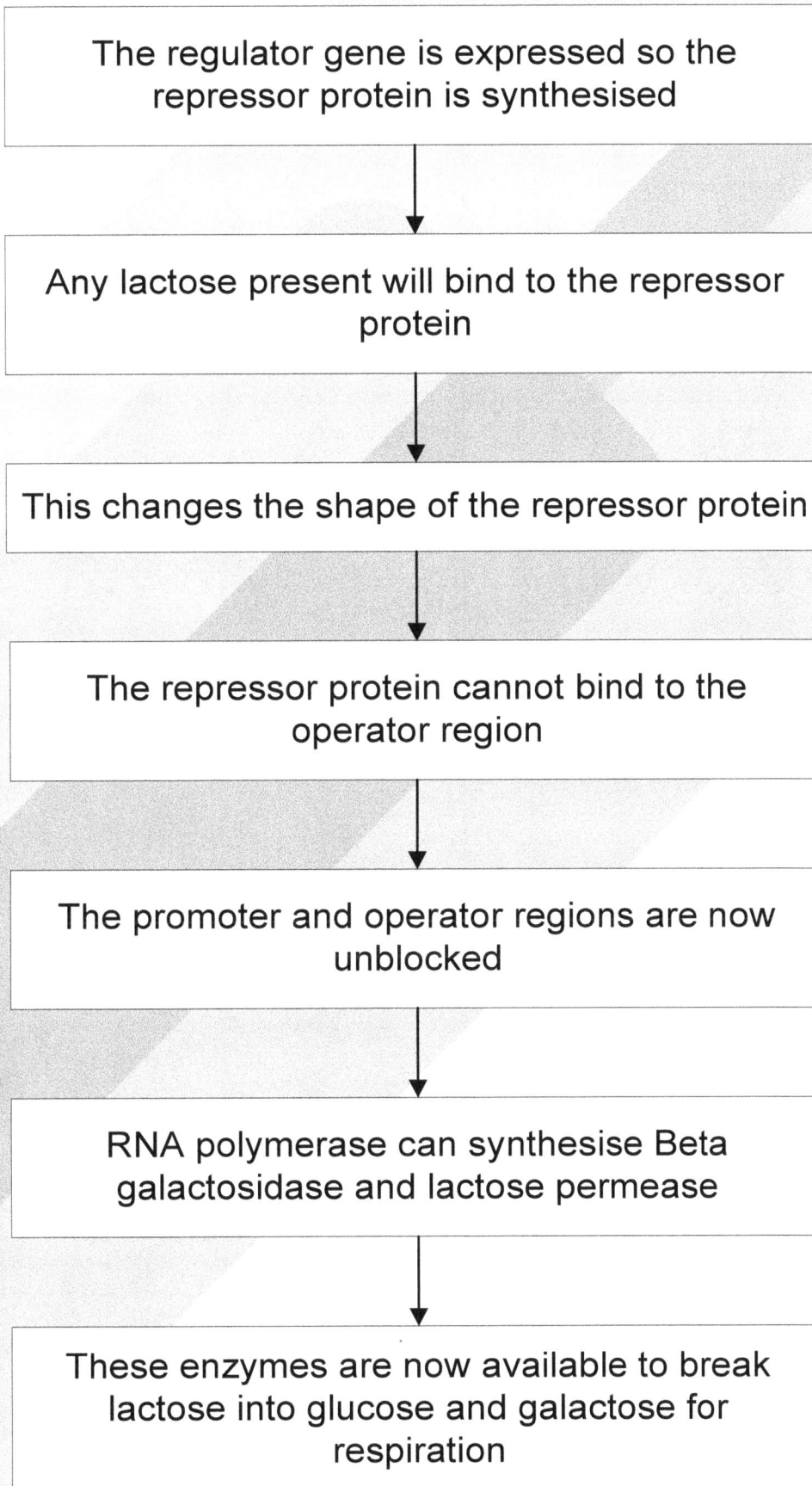

Control of Gene Expression: Nucleus

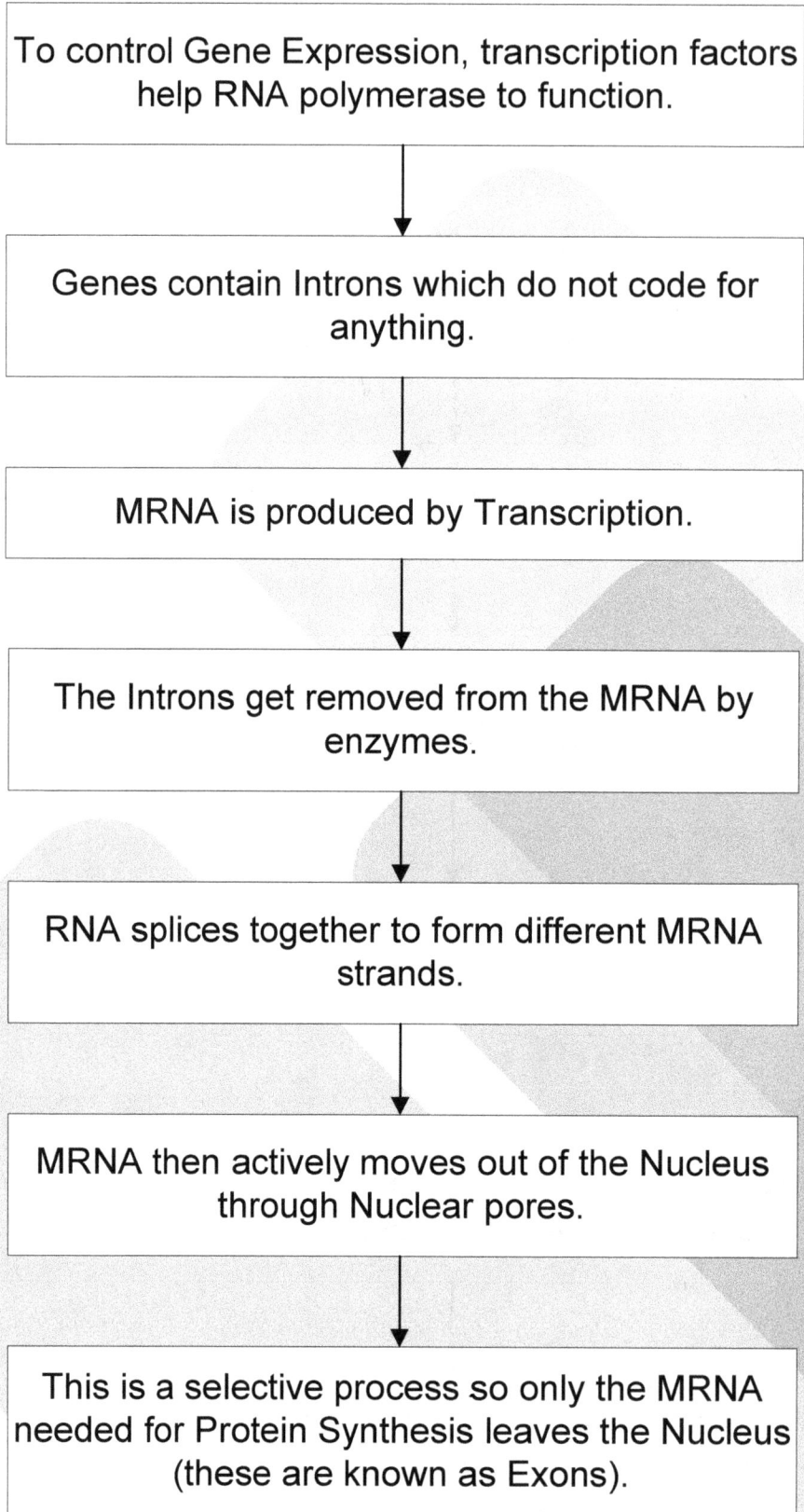

To control Gene Expression, transcription factors help RNA polymerase to function.

↓

Genes contain Introns which do not code for anything.

↓

MRNA is produced by Transcription.

↓

The Introns get removed from the MRNA by enzymes.

↓

RNA splices together to form different MRNA strands.

↓

MRNA then actively moves out of the Nucleus through Nuclear pores.

↓

This is a selective process so only the MRNA needed for Protein Synthesis leaves the Nucleus (these are known as Exons).

revision academy

Ribosomes move along MRNA strands in the Cytoplasm.

↓

Amino Acids are bonded together via Peptide bonds.

↓

Polypeptides are formed.

↓

Post-transcriptional modification is made to the Proteins by enzymes.

↓

The Protein then becomes active.

The Cell Cycle

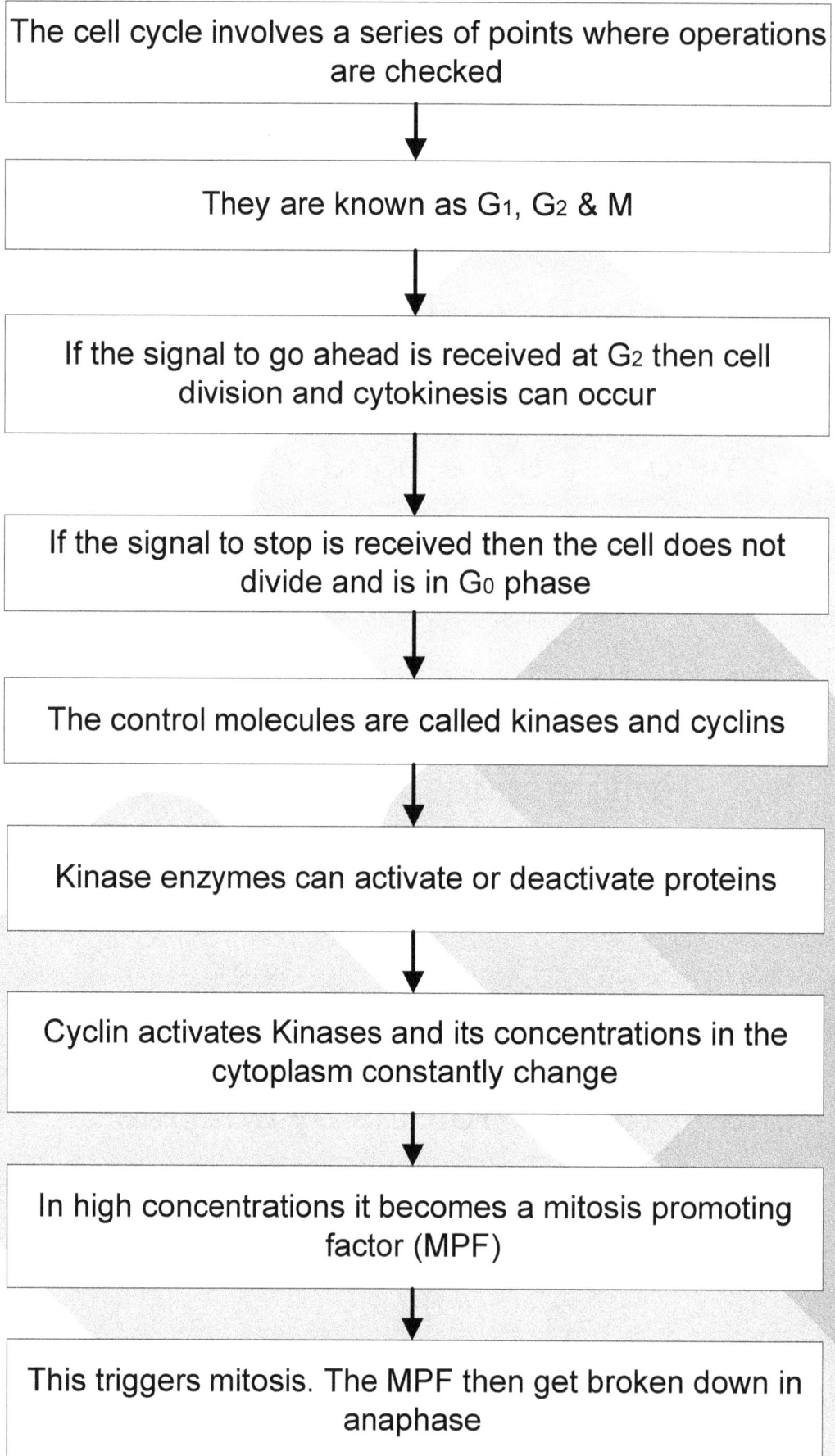

The cell cycle involves a series of points where operations are checked

↓

They are known as G_1, G_2 & M

↓

If the signal to go ahead is received at G_2 then cell division and cytokinesis can occur

↓

If the signal to stop is received then the cell does not divide and is in G_0 phase

↓

The control molecules are called kinases and cyclins

↓

Kinase enzymes can activate or deactivate proteins

↓

Cyclin activates Kinases and its concentrations in the cytoplasm constantly change

↓

In high concentrations it becomes a mitosis promoting factor (MPF)

↓

This triggers mitosis. The MPF then get broken down in anaphase

Water moves from the high water potential soil solution into the root hair cell down a water potential gradient by Osmosis.

↓

Water then moves through the three pathways,
Apoplast – through the cell wall.
Symplast – through Cytoplasm, Plasmodesmata.
Vacuolar – through the Vacuoles.

↓

At the Xylem the Casparian strip exists which prevents the use of the Apoplast pathway.

↓

Salts are actively transported into the Xylem to reduce the water potential within it.

↓

Water moves into the Xylem by Osmosis, this creates root pressure.

Water Uptake by Plants

FLOW
DIAGRAMS

Stages of Drug Testing

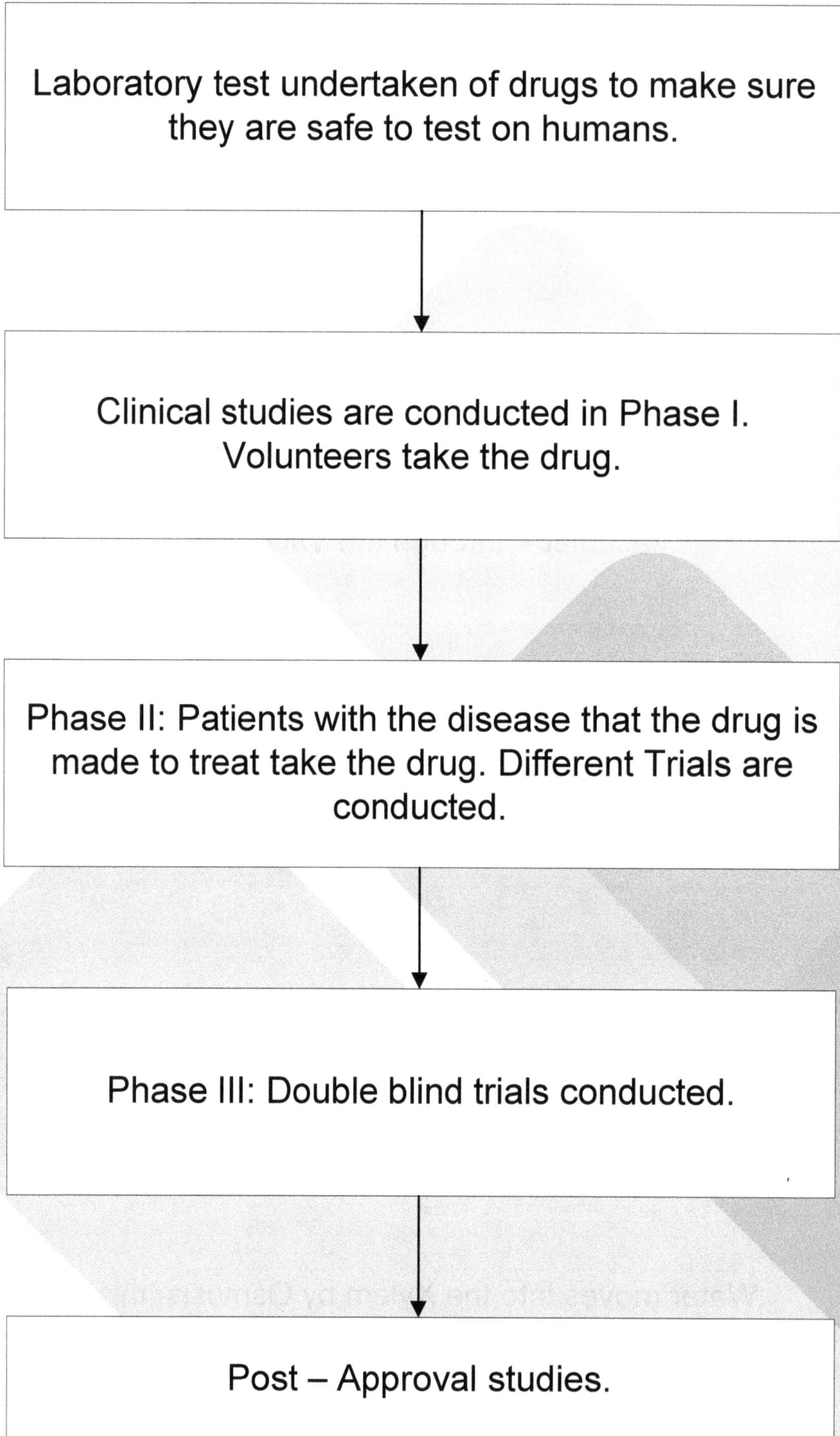

Laboratory test undertaken of drugs to make sure they are safe to test on humans.

Clinical studies are conducted in Phase I. Volunteers take the drug.

Phase II: Patients with the disease that the drug is made to treat take the drug. Different Trials are conducted.

Phase III: Double blind trials conducted.

Post – Approval studies.

revision academy

Bacteria with an Antibiotic resistance are treated with Antibiotics.

↓

The resistance occurs through mutation, conjugation, or when they are infected by a virus.

↓

The resistant Bacteria is not destroyed by the Antibiotic and reproduces.

↓

A new population of Antibiotic resistant Bacteria emerges.

↓

This can happen in many cases.

↓

Overuse and misuse of Antibiotics encourages Antibiotic resistant Bacteria.

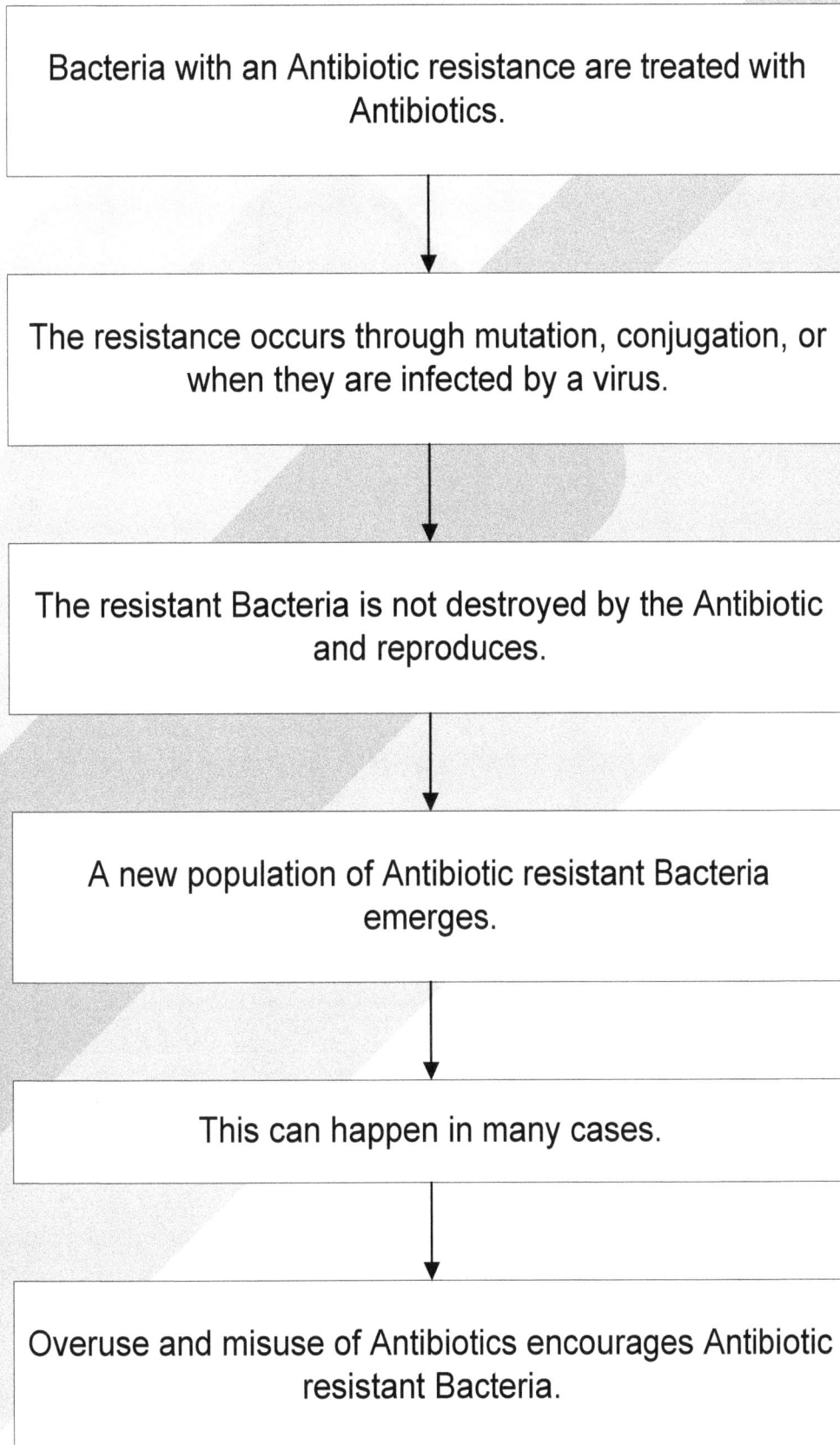

Formation of the Cell Wall

Golgi apparatus produces vesicles, ER secretes wall forming enzymes

↓

These move to the middle line

↓

The first layer forms the middle lamella from calcium pectate

↓

A layer of cellulose is added which forms the primary wall

↓

More layers of cellulose are added to form the secondary wall

↓

In some cell walls lignin is added which hardens the wall

revision academy

Memory Spider Diagram Topics

Here you will find a list of the key topics in the module. For each of these topics you can construct memory spider diagrams every couple of weeks to track the progress of your knowledge.

To do this, take a piece of paper and put the title of the topic in the middle of the page in black pen.

Then, without the aid of any text books or your notes, in black pen write down everything you can remember about that topic.

Once you cannot remember anymore, find the chapter concerning that topic in your text books and notes and look up the information that you missed.

In red pen add the missed out material to your spider diagram.

Keep your spider diagram for your records and use it to compare to subsequent diagrams that you construct on the same subject to show the proportion of black to red and see how you are progressing.

Memory Spider Diagram Topics

- Cell structure (including organelles)

- Prokaryotes & Eukaryotes

- Cell Cycle & Division

- Reproduction

- Stem Cells

- Medical Therapies

- Gene Expression

- Plant Cells

- Plant Tissues

- Water Uptake & Transpiration

- Inorganic Ions In Plants

- Plants & Economics

- Biodiversity

- Classification / Taxonomy

- Adaptations

- Conservation

revision academy

Answers

All the answers to the basic questions and linked topic questions can be found in this section.

ANSWERS

Cell Ultrastructure

1. Cells are the smallest unit of life and the building blocks of life and all cells arise from the division of older cells. They also are the place of all metabolic processes

2. It uses a beam of electrons which passes through the stained biological material and an image is focussed on a fluorescent screen.

3. An electron gun which emits the electron beam, condenser focuses the beam, air lock to introduce specimen, objective that focuses the image, projector which magnifies the image, viewing port, fluorescent screen, camera chamber and a vacuum pump.

4. TEM the electrons pass through the specimen, and SEM pass the electron beam over the top of the specimen to see surface detail.

5. Resolution is when two separate points are distinguishable, the magnification tells us the number of times bigger the image of the specimen is.

6. Eukaryotic cells have membrane bound organelles and prokaryotes do not, and eukaryotic cells are much larger.

7. The sum of all chemical reactions of an organism.

8. The fluid that surrounds organelles.

9. Nuclear membrane that contains pores, it contains a nucleolus and DNA and is used to provide the template for all proteins within the organism.

10. The site of cellular respiration, they have a double membrane, the inner membrane being folded upon itself (cristae) to provide a large surface area for production of ATP.

11. Rough endoplasmic reticulum has ribosomes attached to its single folded membrane where protein synthesis occurs. Vesicles can also be formed when swellings are pinched off from the membrane. Smooth ER is where lipids are manufactured and storage of calcium ions for specific metabolic processes.

12. This is made of sacs that have been flattened formed from the vesicles of ER. This is where some hormones and enzymes are synthesised here and get packaged into vesicles where they are able to be transported around or out of the cell. Some of which are lysosomes.

13. These are vesicles that contain digestive enzymes which can fuse with other molecules and break them down.

14. Microtubules help to move things around in the cell and are made of tubulin which makes them straight and unbranched, centrioles are formed from microtubules and are involved in cell division.

15. Normally bacterial cells so are unicellular and their DNA is free within the cell, they do not contain mitochondria and are very small.

Organisms from Cells

1. A unicellular organism is made of just one cell and multicellular organism is made of many cells.
2. These are the differences between specialised cells.
3. A tissue is many similar specialised cells working together to perform a function and an organ is many different tissues working together to perform a function.
4. There are two growth phases where organelles grow and metabolism takes place and then preparation for cell division and also a synthesis stage where DNA is replicated.
5. Chromatin shortens and thickens to visible chromosomes and the nuclear envelope begins to break down.
6. The spindle fibres form from microtubules and chromosomes line up on the equator attached to the spindle fibres at their centromeres.
7. The spindle fibres begin to shorten pulling the chromosomes apart towards the poles.
8. The nuclear envelopes begin to reform around the chromosomes.
9. This is when the cytoplasm of the cell divides forming two new cells.
10. By completing a root tip squash and staining the cells and observing under a microscope.
11. Two diploid daughter cells.
12. Due to DNA replication in interphase and are divided equally into each of the new cells.
13. For growth and repair and asexual reproduction.
14. It is coiled into chromosomes.

Reproduction in Organisms

1. Asexual reproduction involves cloning the parent cells, only one parent is involved. Sexual reproduction involves genetic material from two parents come together to form a new genetically different individual.

2. Mitosis produces 2 daughter identical cells with a diploid number of chromosomes through one division. Meiosis produces 4 genetically different daughter cells with a haploid number of chromosomes through 2 divisions.

3. Crossing over and random assortment.

4. During meiosis 1.

5. Formed in the testes, they have a head section that contains the nucleus, and an acro some which contains enzymes which break down the membrane of the egg cell, their mid section contains many mitochondria to produce ATP for moving the tail section which is made of microtubules. The sperm must reach an egg and fuse with it to form a zygote.

6. A secondary oocyte contains an egg cell, it coats the egg with follicle cells which the sperm must penetrate in order to reach the nucleus of the egg and fertilise it.

7. See the flow diagram on page 81.

8. When pollen from an anther is transferred to a stigma.

9. Self – pollen from the same plant pollinates its own stigmas, cross – when pollen from a different plant pollinates a different plants stamens.

10. Stamens contain anthers and filaments which contain pollen and are the male parts of the plant, carpels contain an ovary, stigma and style and are the female parts of the plant. Pollen is used to pollinate and fertilise the stigma, and ultimately the ovary of the plant.

11. See flow diagram on page 82.

12. Important for natural selection, survival of the fittest, evolution.

revision
academy

Embryo growth and development

1. Increase in the number of cells of an organism.
2. An un-specialised cell that may become specialised to any particular function.
3. Embryonic stem cells are capable of differentiating into any type of cell whereas adult stem cells are limited to the type of cell they can become. Embryonic stem cells are most of the embryo, adult stem cells are usually found in bone marrow. Embryonic are pluripotent and adult are multipotent.
4. A stem cell that can develop into any type of cell.
5. When embryonic cells have begun to organise themselves.
6. When the blastocyst buries itself into the uterus lining.
7. Providing the developing foetus with nutrients and taking away waste.
8. Makes sure that they continue to divide and be initiated to differentiate into specific cells that will be taken up by a host's tissue without triggering any adverse affects.
9. Complete the table describing the diseases that stem cell treatment may help to treat.

Disease	Description
Type 1 Diabetes	Beta cells within the pancreas are damaged and unable to produce insulin which means blood glucose levels rise.
Spinal cord injuries	When the nerves within the spine become damaged, and motor function within the organism is disrupted.
Parkinson's disease	The part of the brain concerned with movement is damaged and neurones die, causing problems with movement and muscle stiffness.
Multiple sclerosis	The myelin sheath of neurones is damaged so signals are lost, this affects the patients feeling.
Brain damage	Neurones have died due to loss of oxygen and the brain loses function, this can be brought on by many different things.
Duchenne muscular dystrophy	This is a genetic disease where muscles have a lack of the protein dystrophin. Other proteins are used which stops the muscles from being able to contract properly.
Cardiac muscle damage	This is normally caused by a heart attack, and cardiac muscle has insufficient blood supply which leads to death of cells.
Burns	Depending on the severity of the burn, many layers of skin tissue can be irreparably damaged.

10. See flow diagram on page 85.
11. Extracted from the umbilical cord, or inner cell mass of IVF cells.
12. These are obtained from bone marrow.
13. Details of the issues surrounding the use of stem cells including setting up the Human Fertilisation and Embryology Authority in 1991.
14. People struggling to conceive have the chance to be parents, including cancer sufferers. Embryos can be screened for diseases.

15. Some diseases may be passed to offspring that may have been wiped out with infertility, some embryos get destroyed, multiple pregnancies.
16. Possible to obtain ES cells without damaging the embryo, ES research important for future medicine, spare embryos from IVF would be destroyed anyway.
17. Embryo should have human rights from its creation. All human life is sacred, some believe that nature should not be manipulated. Very expensive.
18. Short length of DNA.
19. When a gene is shown in the organisms characteristic.
20. Synthesises or inhibits the synthesis of lactose enzymes depending on the presence of lactose.
21. Inhibition of protein expression in the absence of lactose, see also flow diagram on page 86.
22. Helps to form RNA from DNA.
23. A gene that does not code for anything.
24. See flow diagram on page 88.
25. See flow diagram on page 89.
26. A characteristic that has a whole value and can be placed in a category.
27. A group of genes that determine a characteristic.
28. The inheritance of phenotypes that are determined by many genes at once.
29. By polygenes and also the effects of the environment.
30. Polygenes that control the expression of melanin.
31. Exposure to UV light.
32. A mutation blocks the formation of tryinosinase and therefore unable to form melanin.
33. Melanin levels, day length, exposure to sun.
34. A group of cells that continually divide by mitosis.
35. Through genetic inheritance, exposure to radiation.
36. See the flow diagram on page 90.
37. When the DNA becomes damaged and the cell cycle is no longer regulated.
38. These genes code for proteins that are involved in stimulating the cell cycle.
39. These genes code for proteins that are involved in suppressing the cell cycle.
40. Viruses can invade cells and directly affect the DNA of the cell triggering tumour formation.
41. It regulates neurotransmitter enzymes, with differing concentrations this can affect how well nervous impulses are conducted across synapses, so can lead to many different disorders.

1. The finite structure of a cell.
2. Nucleus, cell membrane, mitochondria, ribosomes, rough & smooth ER, golgi apparatus, lysosomes, cytoplasm.
3. Plant cells have chloroplasts, a cell wall, a permanent vacuole, they do not have a centrosome, and store carbohydrates as starch, animal cells store carbohydrates as glycogen.
4. Chloroplasts are pigmented with a green colour and undertake photosynthesis; amyloplasts are colourless and store starch.
5. A chloroplast has a double membrane and is a biconvex shape, it contains membranes called thylakoids that stack up to form grana. These contain the chlorophyll for photo synthesis. They also contain starch grains within the stroma in-between the grana.
6. This is a sac filled with fluid with a single membrane for retaining the cells shape.
7. Made of cellulose which is a straight chain molecule made from beta glucose. These chains are able to link via hydrogen bonds forming microfibrils and these microfibrils link together to form macrofibrils.
8. See flow diagram on page 94.
9. The middle lamella is the first part of the cell wall when it is formed and lignin is used to strengthen the wall in fibres such as xylem.
10. Connections between plant cells.
11. Gaps in xylem where water may pass through.

How the plant works

1. Supports leaves and flowers for photosynthesis and reproduction, nutrients and water are also transported along the stem.
2. This contains cells specialised for photosynthesis.
3. This is where plants can absorb water and nutrients from the soil and it also gives the plant stability, anchoring it in the ground.
4. Shows how tissues are distributed within different sections of the plant.
5. Single layer called the epidermis containing vascular tissue which is made up of xylem & phloem, these are arranged in a ring.
6. Single layer called the epidermis containing vascular bundles, mesophyll tissue, specialised for photosynthesis.
7. When a cell is full of water due to osmosis and the pressure in the cell stops any further water entering.
8. The cells that make up the packing tissue in plant stems.
9. Similar to parenchyma but has an extra layer of cellulose at each cell corner.
10. A hollow tube which have lateral reinforced walls containing cellulose and lignin, water is able to move through pits in the walls.
11. Outer structure of the vascular bundle, which are dead and thick through extra layers of cellulose.
12. Dicotyledonous- flowering plants with veins in leaves that cross ion different directions. Monocotyledonous- strap shaped leaves with parallel veins.
13. Used in photosynthesis and for structure.
14. Prevents water loss from leaves as it is water proof.
15. Allows water and gases to pass in and out of the plant.
16. Through the root hair cells by osmosis as the water potential withing the root hair cells is lower than that of the soil.
17. The net movement of water in a plant from root to tip along xylem vessels.
18. Calcium for plant cell walls, phosphates for nucleic acids, sulphur and nitrogen for amino acids, magnesium in chlorophyll.

How plants are used

1. Dead plants from the carboniferous period that contained a large amount of carbon through photosynthesis and became fossilised.
2. Food industry, medicine, science, timber, rubber, perfume.
3. Surface fibres, bast fibres, hard fibres, wood fibres
4. Surface fibres: textiles, Bast fibres: Textiles, brush fibres for carpets and rope, hard fibres: brush fibres for mats, wood fibres: paper and cardboard.
5. Used for food, paper, cardboard, building materials, adhesives, cleaning materials, cosmetics, nutrients for micro-organisms, integrated with plastics.
6. Bracken uses chemicals within its cells to deter grazers, these properties could be used or copied for human benefits.
7. It produces a natural insecticide called terpene. This harms insects that attack the plant. This has been extracted from the plants and is used commercially as an insecticide.
8. Garlic: allicin, horse mint: methol and carvone.
9. Can be used as placebos and remedies, and extracted for medicine.
10. Se drug testing flow diagram.
11. Experimented on extracts from the fox glove plant. He suffered from TB, he tested many remedies on his patients until he got successful results. Early form of drug testing.

The Environment and Biodiversity

1. Abundance of different types of species.
2. Group of organisms that can breed and produce fertile offspring.
3. Classification of diversity of organisms.
4. Two part naming system to distinguish between organisms.
5. Using the name of their genus and species.
6. Kingdom, phylum, class order, family, genus, species
7. Place where the majority of species occur.
8. An organism that is restricted to a particular geographical region.
9. Plate tectonics, islands.
10. An area where an organism lives.
11. Abiotic: non biological factor of an environment, Biotic: biological factor of an environment.
12. Measures the biodiversity of a habitat.
13. The alleles of the genes of individuals within a population.
14. Small population of breeding individuals.
15. Study of living things within their environment.
16. Gives information on how an organism feeds and how it behaves with other organisms.
17. Changing their characteristics to best suit the environmental pressures put upon them.
18. Changing their behaviour to best suit the environmental pressures put upon them.
19. Changes in body structure to suit the environment.
20. Where individuals are able to pass on their genes to younger generations by being successful and surviving over other individuals.
21. Can be seen among simpler organisms such as bacteria.
22. Prokaryotes, Protoctista, Fungi, Plants, Animals.
23. An organism that has adapted to survive within extreme environments.
24. The three major forms of life, archaea, bacteria eukarya.
25. Archaea: extremophiles, Bacteria: true bacteria, Eukarya: all eukaryotes.
26. When all organisms from a particular species have died. Caused by predation or extreme events etc.
27. Usually an increase of extinction rate as human population increases.
28. Managing ecosystems to keep a balance despite human interference.
29. Major deforestation.
30. List of endangered species around the world.
31. Practically maintaining and ensuring that species are protected and survive.
32. Selected land that has been set aside as a conservation area. This will have many restrictions of human activity to ensure the species flourish with it.
33. Conservation of a species out of its natural environment.
34. Conservation of a species within its natural habitat.
35. Advantages: Able to keep genetic records of rare and endangered species. The animals live longer and can breed for longer. Attempts are made to re-introduce endangered species back into their habitats. Easy for the public to access and be educated about conservation and different species.
    Disadvantages: Can cause the animals to become stressed. Young do not grow up in their natural habitat and so are unable to learn behaviours properly. Introducing endangered species can be difficult.

revision academy

36. Advantages: The animals are able to live in their natural environment. Monitoring of the reserve area can prevent further decline of the habitat. Offspring will grow up in their natural habitat. People are able to visit the reserves and see animals in their natural habitat. Good place to return engendered species from ex-situ conservation. Disadvantages: Rare habitats are easily lost. When a habitat is lost, the whole community is lost, adding to endangered species numbers.

37. What are the steps needed in creating a seed bank? The seeds must be dried, then packaged in moisture proof containers. The seeds must be stored at temperatures of -18° C. The seeds are checked periodically for their germination. The seeds are re placed periodically.

Linked Topic Question Answers

1. **How does the structure of a plant cell relate to the structure of a plant as a whole?**

   Cellulose cell wall impregnated with lignin.

   Provides support for each plant cell.

   Many plant cells making up tissue contribute to plant structure and stability, particularly within the stem.

   Permanent vacuoles allow individual cells to become turgid.

   This aids again with structure within the plant.

2. **How does meiosis help to maintain biodiversity?**

   Having different parents with different genes leads to variation.

   Genetic material from a sperm and an egg.

   During Meiosis 1 chromosomes cross over. Crossing over means change in the chromosomes. Chromosomes line up at random along the equator.

   Random assortment means differences in the genetic material of daughter cells.

   This produces variation within organisms.

   Different organisms will be able to survive different selection pressures.

   This helps to maintain the population of each species.

3. **How can biodiversity be increased?**

   Use of in-situ and ex-situ conservation plans.

   Organisms can be encouraged to breed with one another.

   Manipulating genes in the lab and incorporating them with genes of different individuals.

   Subjecting different organisms to different selection pressures.

   This causes organisms to adapt.

   As a result variation within genetic material is increased.

4. **Why are plants so important?**

   Plants are a food source for many organisms.

   Plants can be used in industry for many different purposes, from medicines to using their fibres for clothing.

   Plants harvest light energy from the sun and produce their own food source.

   This is the basis or most of life on Earth.

   Plants therefore support nearly all living organisms on Earth.

5. **How can cell specialisation be used in medicine?**

   Stem cells are cells that have not yet specialised.

   These stem cells can be manipulated to continue to proliferate.

   They can then be induced to differentiate into specific cells types.

   These can be integrated within patients suffering particular diseases.

   They are then checked to maintain they are functioning correctly.

   They must also be checked that they do not cause adverse effects within the individual.

revision academy

Acknowledgements

Special thanks to Ben Richardson for proof reading and checking through the workbook.
We would also like to thank Amanda Mann for help with data input.

The author and the publisher would like to thank the following for permission to reproduce the following images:

Cover: Knorre / shutterstock
p.8: Synthus design
p.12: Maxi_m / shutterstock
p.16: zuzazuz / shutterstock
p.20: somersault1824 / shutterstock
p.29: Synthus design
p.33: Synthus design
p.38: molekuul.be / shutterstock
p.42: red_frog / istock
p.110: dream designs / shutterstock; Mopic / shutterstock; Maya 2008 / shutterstock

Also in this series.......

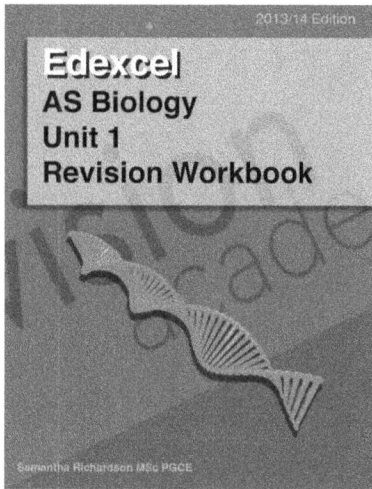

Edexcel
AS Biology
Unit 1
Revision Workbook

ISBN 978-1-910060-04-9

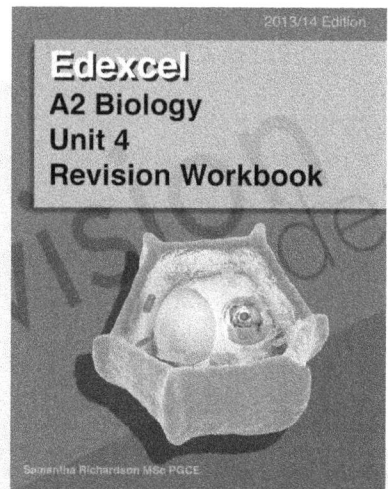

Edexcel
A2 Biology
Unit 4
Revision Workbook

ISBN 978-1-910060-06-3

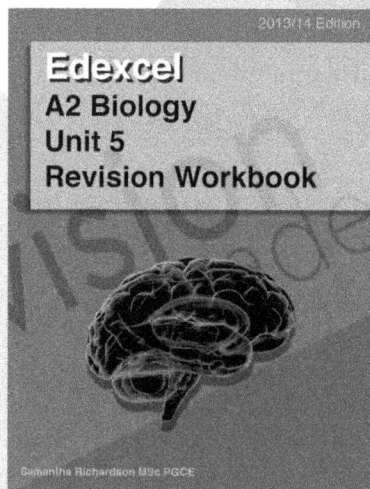

Edexcel
A2 Biology
Unit 5
Revision Workbook

ISBN 978-1-910060-07-0

Synthus
Publishing

www.synthus.co.uk

revision academy

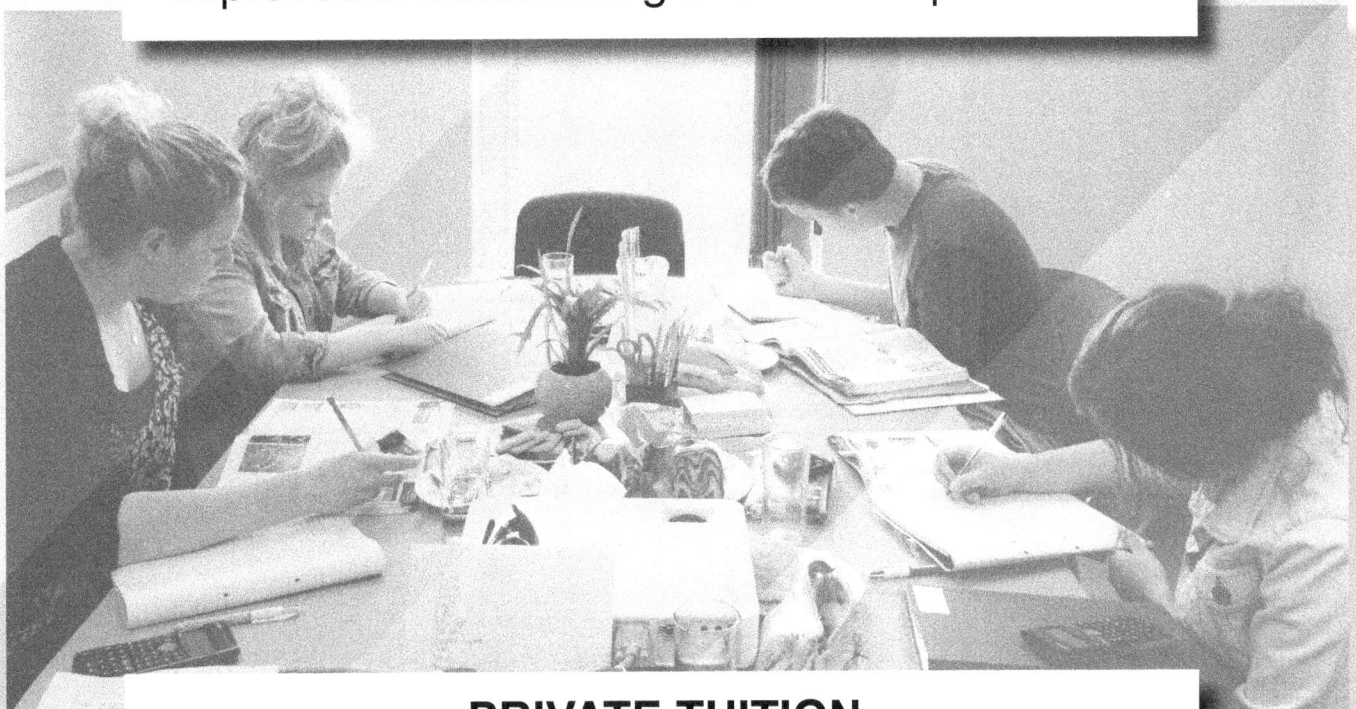

www.ingramcontent.com/pod-product-compliance
Lightning Source LLC
Chambersburg PA
CBHW080608090426
42735CB00017B/3369